5

PSALMIST'S CRY

scripts for embracing lament

Copyright 2010
by The House Studio and The Work of the People

ISBN 978-0-8341-2593-3

Printed in the United States of America

Cover Design, Interior Design and Photography by Brandon Hill, bhilldesign.com

thehousestudio.com

10 9 8 7 6 5 4 3 2 1

WALTER BRUEGGEMANN

WITH STEVE FROST

PSALMIST'S CRY

scripts for embracing lament

CONTENTS

INTRODUCTION

I had an older brother named Judson. He lived for only a few minutes after he was born, and then he was gone. One of my family's stories is about the doctor who told my dad, in an offhanded, matter-of-fact sort of way, that his infant son was gone. Maybe of all the tragedies the doctor saw that day, this event was the least tragic. Maybe he had seen too much death and had grown callous. Maybe he had no time for emotion.

I'm not sure how my parents grieved Judson's death, but I think they did the best they could, and their lives went on. For their 50th wedding anniversary, I made them a book, lovingly editing hundreds of old family pictures. It was a strangely intimate process—zooming in at 300%, gently brushing away the digital dust from familiar faces.

I had only one picture of Judson to work with—his funeral picture. I knew about the *idea* of my brother. But I had never really confronted *losing* him. As I worked on the picture, tears began to flow. As my digital pen caressed his cheek, his eye, I was connected to my brother in a way I had never been. Eventually I had to stop working. I just sat in front of my computer and wept. After all these years, I finally grieved my brother, alone in front of my computer.

I had never let the reality of my older brother in, and so I had nothing to lose. Now, as the possibilities came flooding in, with them came the mourning of those possibilities that never were. I remember thinking, what kind of culture do I live in that grief and lament are so foreign?

You might think, what does this have to do with me? Is this just another self-help book? Maybe you've never lost anyone close to you. But surely there have been points in your life when you haven't felt like praising God. When your parents divorced. Or when you experienced the death of your own relationship. When your dream job—or any job—became a memory of a time when you weren't relying on unemployment checks to get by.

Whatever your unique story, none of us can deny that we live in a society uncomfortable with lament. Our self-help, pop-a-pill culture convinces us there's a solution to every problem. We just need to find, or buy, the right one. So we tuck our lament safely away in the pockets of clinical lab coats. We hand our human emotions to professionals, thinking a calm veneer of expertise will stand in for honest lament.

But as Christians, when we lose lament we lose more than the journey of a full human experience. When we skip lament altogether, heading straight for praise, we fail to identify with Jesus Christ, who is not only our savior and the son of our creator God but was also fully man, walking the same earth we do. The man who suffered more than any of us can fathom. And we lose the depth and goodness of the gospel.

This is why I'm so thankful for theologian Walter Brueggemann, whose work unlocks the Psalms as scripts for embracing lament. We can look to the Psalms for guidance in the abandoned moments of our lives, when we need to honestly cry out to God in ways and words not generally accepted by our society—and Christian culture. If we allow them to, psalms become more than a few lines of praise we recite at church each week; they can become a guide for moving past our denial, honestly engaging our lament and arriving at genuine praise.

DENIAL

What breaks your heart?

I think that national church leaders do not project the dynamism or the danger or the goodness of the gospel. I sit in a little safe place, so I probably shouldn't criticize people like that who have such huge responsibilities that I don't even understand. **But I just think that there is a revolution going on in our society that makes it exactly the right time for the gospel.** It's so easy to get caught in business as usual about this and miss what's going on, I think.

What is the gospel? Do you really believe in all these books, or is it just a way to generate some cash?

Both. It's both. I had a very senior colleague at Columbia Seminary who was adored by everyone. He was a Barthian. In a pensive moment in a faculty meeting one day, he said, "what if all this isn't true?" So I do think that sometimes, and then I think that I'm a huckster. I believe it, but I'm something of a coward about my own life, and I know that because I'm very comfortable, very middle class, and I don't want to run very great risks. So I often think about the confessing church in Germany and all those people and I wonder often where I would be about that.

If you could do things over again, would you change anything? What would you change?

I think I would…I grew up in a parsonage, and I spent a lot of my time measuring up and doing the right thing. And I wish much earlier in life that I'd claimed more freedom than I claimed. I used too much of my energy away from that. So I've done a huge amount of personal work in the last decade of processing that, which means I did it very late in my life. I'm going to be seventy-six next week, and I wish I had known so much earlier. But I also know there is a time to know and a time not to know, and you cannot rush the process.

Meaning he studied and subscribed to the theology of Karl Barth, a 20th-century Swiss theologian.

Brueggemann is referring to the German church during World War II. The national church submitted to Adolf Hitler while the confessing church treasured Christ.

DISCUSSION QUESTIONS

1

How do we keep ourselves safe, avoid taking risks? In what ways do you think we avoid the danger of the gospel?

2

If church leaders, along with all Christians, began to project the dynamism and danger of the gospel, how would this change affect how we live as Christians? How we interact with culture? How we interact with each other?

COMMENTARY

In this video, Brueggemann discusses his belief that the dynamism, danger, and goodness of the gospel are not being properly projected in our churches. We might ask, "What is dangerous about the gospel?" But, perhaps before answering this question, we should ask, "What *is* the gospel?"

In as much as the gospel is the "good news," the story that God, as Jesus, walked among us, died, and was raised, it is also the story of a life *lived*—here and now, incarnate, in the flesh. It is the whole depth and breadth of the heart, soul, mind, and body of the liver of that life, Jesus. While it was a life marked by beautiful friendship, love and laughter, it was also one marked by weeping and deep pain. Jesus was the resurrected savior, but he was also "despised and rejected by men, a man of sorrows, and familiar with suffering" (Isaiah 53:3).

Perhaps then, this is the danger in the gospel Brueggemann is referring to—that along with the hope and promise of new life come the realization that new life comes out of death (John 12:23-25). New life grows out of the soil of an honest engagement with our own deep pain. But not just our deep pain, the deep pain of a broken world manifest in the faces and places of our own neighborhoods.

For some of us, Brueggemann gives words to our internal fears about the danger of the gospel when he says, "I'm something of a coward about my own life, and I know that. Because I'm very comfortable and very middle class and I don't want to run very great risks." Deep down, I too am fearful and anxious about my own life. I'm afraid to think too deeply about new life coming out of death. Like most people, I have a healthy fear of death. I know Jesus called me to die to myself, and I know the world I hope for, the one Jesus talked about as being the kingdom of God, will come about only when I do die to myself. But most of the time I live in a tension between the knowledge that life comes out of death and my inherent fear of having to personally experience anything too uncomfortable, too difficult, too sacrificial. Too death-like.

I know my "go to" tactic for dealing with the tension between my fear and the world I hope for is denial. I deny my longing for the fullness of God's kingdom and convince myself I have everything I want—or that I can obtain everything I need. I convince myself that being married (or single), having the latest gadget, a better car, a different career, more vacation time, a bigger (or smaller) house, or any number of obtainable things, will be enough. Denial isn't conscious or intended; it's just what I know. My culture gives me a whole lot of help in knowing how to live in denial.

A Culture of Image

For instance, this video series is, at its core, image. We tend to forget this fact in our culture because ours is a culture of image.[1] Image is the air we breathe. As you watch these videos, you aren't *talking to* Brueggemann; you are watching an *image of* Brueggemann. As such, each video is mediated, meaning you are not directly experiencing the full personhood of Brueggemann as he was on the day of filming. Instead, an intermediary, the filmmaker, has added his or her vision, skill, talent, hopes, weaknesses, foibles, and agenda to an actual encounter with Brueggemann. The mediated reality of these videos is a constructed reality with a distinct editorial voice.

This revelation is neither new nor, in and of itself, bad; it's just the reality of media. The mediated nature of our media (think about those two words) is something we rarely consider—or even notice. It is a dynamic underlying novels, the evening news, and everything in between. All the media we encounter is, at its core, a mediated and constructed reality. Reality TV presents itself as unedited veracity—the way things *really* are. The evening news presents itself as fact. But anyone even remotely familiar with TV production knows reality TV is anything but real, and objective news is certainly not objective. Honest filmmakers will acknowledge that simply pointing the camera in one direction rather than another is an editorial act—which is dangerous only when we forget it is true.

[1] See for example Daniel J. Boorstin, *The Image: A Guide to Pseudo-Events in America* (New York: Atheneum, 1987); Neil Postman, *Technopoly: The Surrender of Culture to Technology* (New York: Knopf, 1992); and Neil Gabler, *Life: The Movie: How Entertainment Conquered Reality* (New York: Knopf, 1998).

The filmic medium is the *lingua franca,*[2] the universal language, of our culture—and it speaks powerfully to us. At its best it connects us, as viewers, to our shared humanity. The filmic medium is at its most powerful when we are fully aware of what it is (a film, a TV show), and it connects as media to our humanity in such a way that we change for the better in our day-to-day interactions with other humans.

However, media is at its worst when it presents itself as *other* or *more than* what it is. It is at its worst when it intentionally (or unintentionally) stands in for the open-ended, mysterious interaction negotiated between two human beings. The media around us becomes insidious when we begin to believe it can stand in for actual human interaction, when we forget that we control how we interact with these images. As long as these encounters are exclusively on our terms, they cannot be authentic person-to-person experiences.

Emotional Inoculation

If we believe human encounters are and should be exclusively on our terms, we might also begin to believe *almost* the real thing is just as good as the risky encounter of real human interaction—or even that almost the real thing *is* a real human interaction. In his book *Thy Kingdom Connected*, Dwight Friesen explains Martin Buber's notion of I & It/I & You relationships. I & It relationships can be between inanimate objects. But I & It

[2]A distinct language used between people not sharing a mother tongue.

relationships can also be between people, when "rather than a genuine encounter, the I sees the other person as an idea, or a conceptualization, and treats that person as an object." In contrast, I & You relationships are "a genuine…encounter, because these persons meet one another in their authentic existence, without any qualification or objectification of one another." Friesen notes, "I sometimes wonder whether part of the allure of websites like Facebook and MySpace is that they promise an I & You encounter for the low price of an I & It relationship."[3]

When we substitute mediated, image-based encounters for human inter-action, we emotionally inoculate ourselves to genuine joy and genuine grief. We inoculate ourselves to the full thickness and richness of our human experience, to our pain and to our neighbor's pain. Having been inoculated to our pain we are fooled into thinking our pain has been dealt with—fooled into thinking it no longer exists. If we are confronted with the uncomfortable notion that perhaps we *are* in pain, we instead defer to the more manageable and comfortable notion that we must not be in light of the experience of emotional inoculation. In short, we deny our pain. If we deny our pain we are left unable to follow Jesus into a life familiar with suffering. Without the full gamut of human emotion, the genuine joy and the genuine grief, we lose the danger of the gospel, and in doing so, we lose the depth of its goodness.

[3] Dwight J. Friesen, *Thy Kingdom Connected: What the Church Can Learn from Facebook, the Internet, and Other Networks* (Grand Rapids, MI: Baker Books 2009), 50-52.

DISCUSSION QUESTIONS

1 Realistically, we can't—nor should we—remove ourselves completely from our media-, image-driven culture. Have you ever felt as though you've lost yourself in a constructed reality? How can we live in our culture without losing ourselves in it?

2 Do you think human interactions have become more difficult because we hide behind *almost* human interaction? Why or why not? Is it easier to emotionally disconnect when you avoid genuine human interaction?

We sometimes forget that in his life on earth, Jesus experienced a full scope of emotion. Do we lose the depth of the gospel and fail to identify with Christ when we don't also experience genuine joy and genuine grief?

Read Psalm 88 aloud, as a public expression—
as Israel would have done.

Psalm 88

O LORD, the God who saves me,
day and night I cry out before you.
May my prayer come before you;
turn your ear to my cry.
For my soul is full of trouble
and my life draws near the grave.
I am counted among those who go down to the pit;
I am like a man without strength.
I am set apart with the dead,
like the slain who lie in the grave,
whom you remember no more,
who are cut off from your care.
You have put me in the lowest pit,
in the darkest depths.

Your wrath lies heavily upon me;
you have overwhelmed me with all your waves.
You have taken from me my closest friends
and have made me repulsive to them.
I am confined and cannot escape;
my eyes are dim with grief.
I call to you, O LORD, every day;
I spread out my hands to you.
Do you show your wonders to the dead?
Do those who are dead rise up and praise you?
Is your love declared in the grave,
your faithfulness in Destruction?
Are your wonders known in the place of darkness,
or your righteous deeds in the land of oblivion?
But I cry to you for help, O LORD;
in the morning my prayer comes before you.
Why, O LORD, do you reject me
and hide your face from me?
From my youth I have been afflicted and
close to death;
I have suffered your terrors and am in despair.

Your wrath has swept over me;
your terrors have destroyed me.
All day long they surround me like a flood;
they have completely engulfed me.
You have taken my companions and loved ones from me;
the darkness is my closest friend.

Remind your group of God's presence among you, that through Jesus, God knows our pain. Dare to let the honesty and depth of this psalm guide your group past denial. Notice how this psalm ends, and allow room for the same kind of ragged ending to your gathering. As a group, don't rush to closure—this is a necessary first step on what will hopefully be a long journey together.

STATUS QUO

An artist has to seek an audience or a constituency, and I think they are to be found among the wounded. I think the wounded in our society are everywhere, but we are schooled in denial. So I believe the hard task is to break the denial so that people can get in touch with their own pain. I think that art both ministers to people at the point of their pain but may also be a way of penetrating the denial to have a conversation about it in the first place.

I think that the pressure for certitude and absolutism is a kind of an anxious, frightened response to the reality of pain and we think we cannot bear it, so we protect ourselves from it by imagining that we don't know about our own pain. What we always discover is that if we can get access to our pain in a community that we trust, our pain almost always is bearable because the trustworthiness of our brothers and sisters will hold and is reliable and will not let us fall through.

And it seems to me that what good artistry has to do is to help us see or hear that our certitudes are mainly phony, that life does not conform to our certitudes, that our absolutes are much less than absolute because of force of stuff that comes underneath in our experience will not give in to that. So when I think of the Old Testament, I think that Job is the perfect model of that. Job's friends are the practitioners of certitude and absolute orthodoxy and all that, and Job's artistry keeps coming underneath that to protest against that cover up. And I don't quite know how it works in the book of Job, but I believe that God in the whirlwind speeches is also something of an artist, that he moves in big images and questions and invites a fresh think about things. So that seems to me to be a place in which the poetry wants to subvert the world of the prose in which the friends live. So that's how my mind works about it.

And if we think at all about the church, it is historically and intrinsically an artistic operation. It always struck me, in the little rural church where I grew up, that no matter how flat and unimaginative and prosaic the life of the village was, we had that organ music on Sunday morning. And what that organ music did was to create space for us to ponder the stuff that didn't fit the formulii. And by and large, the language of the church and the language of liturgy is essentially artistic language. We flattened it. So the work, it seems to me, first of all is to help people see that what has been entrusted to us is artistic from the bottom up. And if people are caught in dogmatism or in moralism, they tend not to notice how incredibly artistic it all is.

DISCUSSION QUESTIONS

1

Are we really, as Brueggemann says, "schooled in denial?" If yes, what do you think he means by this statement? What are we taught to deny? What are some certitudes we hold on to?

2 Why should we want to access our pain?
What are the benefits, and drawbacks,
of living this way?

COMMENTARY

We are enveloped by a consumer culture that increasingly insists we are generic consumers first and specific people second. Another way of saying this is that to live in our world means primarily being identified mostly by our type—women or men of a certain age, race, religion, and so on. On a large scale, our culture rarely acknowledges the individuality of people on more than a surface level. Brueggemann has called this the culture of "technological, therapeutic, consumer militarism."[4] As generic consumers, and in order for a consumer culture to run smoothly, we must exist in a constant state of expecting or hoping that our deepest desires will be met through the purchasing of goods and services. If we begin to question whether our deepest desires *can* be met through the purchasing of goods and services, or if we begin to acknowledge that our deepest needs have in fact *not* been met through the purchasing of goods and services, we threaten the smooth functioning of consumer culture.

In our consumer culture, negative human emotion isn't actively denied; instead, it's passively ignored, like an unintelligible language of gibberish.

---

[4] Paul Soupiset. "Walter Brueggemann's 19 Theses." http://soupiset.typepad.com/soupablog/Brueggemann_19_Theses.html.

Consumer culture exists solely in a world of manufactured desire, where there is no need for pain: indeed, the idea of pain would be harmful to the process of manufacturing desire. After all, beer commercials would be much less appealing if they were littered with grieving divorcées languishing in seedy bars rather than attractive co-eds playing beach volleyball. In this world, there is no room for reality—only for vivid, perfected pictures of a world we hope for, in which our deepest human desires are met by purchasing and possessing consumer goods.

The Church in Denial

But our Western, consumer-driven culture isn't the only entity teaching us to deny our pain, to avoid lament. In other writings, Brueggemann discusses the centuries-long perpetuation of denial—and the Church's role in it.

> All these denials about endings are necessary in the royal community because it is too costly to face and embrace them. It would suggest that we are not in charge, that things will not forever stay the manageable way they are, and that things will not finally all work out. It is the business of kings to attach the word "forever" to everything we treasure. The great dilemma is that religious functionaries are expected to use the same "forever," to attach it to things and make it sound theologically legitimated. But "forever" is always the word of Pharaoh, and as such it is the very word against which Yahweh and Moses did their liberating thing.[5]

[5] Walter Brueggemann, *The Prophetic Imagination: Second Edition*, (Minneapolis: Augsburg Fortress, 2001), 42.

For Brueggemann, the "royal community" includes anyone who places their future hope in all that the pharaoh of Old Testament Egypt represents—their own power and cleverness, their ability to manage and solve problems, their enduring self-sufficiency. The above quote implicates "religious functionaries" who use the word "forever," attaching it to theological language. It makes us feel better to simply say that God has always been and will forever be God. To understand an incomprehensible God, we use certain, absolute words like forever, and thus, we strip away the mystery of our creator God, excusing ourselves from considering deeply the nature of who he is.

Brueggemann believes certitude—a certainty greater than circumstances warrant—and absolutism are an anxious response to the reality of pain. A voice of certitude is one that claims to control the means by which we might be safe and happy. In order to deliver safety and happiness, the voice of certitude must be in control of—or appear to be in control of—any situation that potentially impinges upon safety and happiness. This language of control is one of categorizing, measuring, and analyzing. Mystery, precisely because it can't be categorized, measured, or analyzed, cannot be controlled. Thus, mystery is a perceived threat to the voice of certitude's pretense of delivering safety and happiness. In a world dominated by the voice of certitude there is no room for mystery, and therefore no room for the God of the Bible who remains, above all, a vibrant dynamic mystery.

In contrast to the voice of certitude, Brueggemann presents the voice of fidelity—faithfulness—and characterizes Yahweh, the God of the Bible, as an enduring voice of fidelity. Fidelity isn't governed by control, certitude or absolutism; it is governed by *hesed*, *mishpat* and *tsedika*— steadfast love, the right use of power and a commitment to restore all relationships. Fidelity isn't a commitment to control; it is a commitment to stay with us no matter what. Fidelity is a characteristic of love. A commitment to fidelity brings all kinds of risks: in the matter of love, it risks the indifference of the one who is loved; in justice it risks the possibility of violence; and in righteousness, fidelity risks being rejected. Most of all, fidelity risks the future. In refusing to control and instead committing to "be with," fidelity leaves the future wide open to infinite possibility. Fully free persons move from possibility to possibility, together.

Certitude reveals anxiousness in our lives because it refuses the risky possibilities of fidelity. As a response to pain in particular, fidelity acknowledges pain and embraces the risky possibility of love, justice, and righteousness in the hope of a future in which our pain, through the mysterious transforming power of Yahweh, might become joy. Certitude, without a language to understand mystery, can't understand the possibilities offered through mystery. Instead, certitude anxiously attempts to control future possibility by denying pain. If there is no pain, there is no need to risk safety and happiness for the sake of transformation.

Brueggemann has argued in many places[6] that the rule of King Solomon is a critical turning point in the history of Israel. Under Solomon's rule Israel leaves behind the God-dependent vitality of Moses that had been at its core and instead moves toward a self-dependent security provided by a self-interested royal community: it is interested in its continued existence above all else, especially above justice and compassion. Because of its self-interest, it is occupied by control, which in turn leads it to be occupied by fear of losing control.

In a context bent on control, unanswered questions are dangerous, creating the drive for certitude and absolutism. No question can go unanswered, no problem unsolved. This frantic push toward certitude is driven by fear—fear of losing control. The push toward certitude refuses to abide in the mystery of Yahweh, but instead, out of anxious fear, pretends to be resolved toward an action regardless of how effective that resolution might actually be. In personal terms, if we refuse to abide in our pain and anxiously deny our pain or move on to control our pain, we preempt God's moving, eliminating the space in which God might minister to us.

---

[6] See Brueggemann's *The Prophetic Imagination* (Minneapolis: Augsburg Fortress, 1978); *Finally Comes the Poet: Daring Speech for Proclamation* (Minneapolis: Augsburg Fortress, 1989); and most forcefully at *The Church in Joyous Obedience: Biblical Expositions* (Regent College Laing Lectures 2008), found at http://www.regentbookstore.com/product_details.php?item_id=52252&category_id=513.

DISCUSSION QUESTIONS

1   In a consumer culture in which negative emotion is ignored and we're told there's no need for pain, how can we access our pain in genuine, authentic ways?

2   How has the contemporary church become like a royal community—embracing self-sufficiency and certitude? How does operating as a royal community strip God of God's artistry and mystery? Why do you think we tend to attach absolutes to God?

3

Do you ever wish you could pin God down? Do you think trying to find all the answers prevents God from moving in our midst? Is our faith actually enhanced when we embrace the mystery of God rather than imposing our limits on him?

Read Psalm 44 aloud as a public expression.

Psalm 44

We have heard with our ears, O God;
our fathers have told us
what you did in their days,
in days long ago.
With your hand you drove out the nations
and planted our fathers;
you crushed the peoples
and made our fathers flourish.
It was not by their sword that they won the land,
nor did their arm bring them victory;
it was your right hand, your arm,
and the light of your face, for you loved them.
You are my King and my God,
who decrees victories for Jacob.
Through you we push back our enemies;

through your name we trample our foes.
I do not trust in my bow,
my sword does not bring me victory;
but you give us victory over our enemies,
you put our adversaries to shame.
In God we make our boast all day long,
and we will praise your name forever.
But now you have rejected and humbled us;
you no longer go out with our armies.
You made us retreat before the enemy,
and our adversaries have plundered us.
You gave us up to be devoured like sheep
and have scattered us among the nations.
You sold your people for a pittance,
gaining nothing from their sale.
You have made us a reproach to our neighbors,
the scorn and derision of those around us.
You have made us a byword among the nations;
the peoples shake their heads at us.
My disgrace is before me all day long,

and my face is covered with shame
at the taunts of those who reproach and revile me,
because of the enemy, who is bent on revenge.
All this happened to us,
though we had not forgotten you
or been false to your covenant.
Our hearts had not turned back;
our feet had not strayed from your path.
But you crushed us and made us a haunt for jackals
and covered us over with deep darkness.
If we had forgotten the name of our God
or spread out our hands to a foreign god,
would not God have discovered it,
since he knows the secrets of the heart?
Yet for your sake we face death all day long;
we are considered as sheep to be slaughtered.
Awake, O Lord! Why do you sleep?
Rouse yourself! Do not reject us forever.
Why do you hide your face
and forget our misery and oppression?

We are brought down to the dust;
our bodies cling to the ground.
Rise up and help us;
redeem us because of your unfailing love.

Remind each other of God's presence among you, that God already knows the deepest hurt in our hearts. Encourage each other to allow the insight gained in group discussion to enliven, shift, and refresh your understanding of Psalm 44.

BREAKING THE SILENCE

Praise hymns are so bloodless and innocuous. I think they're exercises in denial. I think eventually you get to praise, but as you know, in the book of Psalms, you do the lament and then you, at the end of the psalm, you come to praise, but you don't start there. You never start there.

In the more liturgical churches, I don't know if this is true in evangelical churches, but my gripe about liturgical churches is you always begin with a confession of sin. Most of these lament songs, there's nothing about guilt in them: "You're not going to pin this problem on me." So I think the pastoral work has to do with entitling and empowering people to make a case in the presence of God for the legitimacy of their own life. All kinds of artistry I think is important to do that. For people who are conventional about that, all that obviously feels like blasphemy.

That's why I say the first audience are the most wounded. Because the most wounded have this sneaking suspicion, yeah, we really, we do have to say that. So I would imagine that in any congregation you've probably got the people that need to do this and you've got the silencers. But more than that, I suspect in the life of an individual believer, this same tension is operating because my mother always washed my mouth out if I talked poorly or badly. But I *have* to, and then you have to negotiate how much of this you can say and all that.

So I think that these psalms, they become a script for learning how to speak what we have to say that we were never permitted to say. And then I think all kinds of artistry can do the same thing. But until the hurt or the pain is made available to people, then we can just go on our way with denial, and everything is just fine.

DISCUSSION QUESTIONS

1 Do you agree that praise hymns are "bloodless and innocuous" and are "exercises in denial?" Why or why not?

2 What harm might exist in starting with praise rather than arriving at praise through lament?

Have you ever used psalms the way Brueggemann describes—as scripts to cry out to God when no other words seem adequate? Can you remember a time in your life when using psalms as scripts might have helped get you through to genuine praise?

COMMENTARY

In this video Brueggemann talks about the idea of our "pain being made available" to us as an agent of healing and change. Our culture tends to contradict this claim. It tells us all problems are solvable, or at least manageable; we simply need to try (or buy) the right solution. At my local grocery store, for instance, there are seemingly innumerable varieties of headache medicines. Logically then, there are an endless number of solutions to all my headache problems. If I remain afflicted with a headache, I'm at fault for not finding what must surely be the right painkiller from an exhaustive selection of painkilling solutions.

Actually, though, pain*killers* all contain one of the same few ingredients and do more or less the exact same thing—mask pain. In truth, our self-help, pop-a-pill culture is prone to masking symptoms and calling that mask a cure; we aren't very good at dealing with whatever caused the symptom in the first place. This is especially true of emotional pain.

In such a context we might be quick to question Brueggemann, to be skeptical that we require access to pain in order that we might change. What pain could we really experience anyway? Most of us lack nothing—we aren't without food or shelter, we have our own (maybe even multiple) cars, TVs, movies, the internet, and iPhones. We have brighter colors, closer shaves, and impossibly white teeth. Where is there room for pain?

Could it be that the process of getting and keeping all these wonderful things creates our isolated, lonely, fragmented lives, our shallow or broken relationships, our deep, abiding pain in our souls? Add into the mix users and abusers, people who dominate, control, and hurt in innumerable ways—people who have been present in every culture at every point in history. For good measure add human brokenness, the ability of every one of us to be a user and abuser, our ability to kill those closest to us with a thousand quiet cuts. In short, our culture provides plenty of opportunity to collect pain, but generally, under the guise of "solutions" that in reality only mask our pain.

The First Step

Before the Psalms can be "a script for learning how to speak what we have to say that we were never permitted to say," our pain must be "made available" to us. How might we begin this process? And why would we *want* to feel pain? To get a handle on what Brueggemann is talking about, it might help to think of ourselves as emotional lepers. Before we can deal with our pain, we first have to be healed of our emotional leprosy. We must access our pain in order to deal honestly with the cause of our pain. We could look to Matthew 8:1-4, a story about Jesus healing a leper, to gain some insight.

First of all, it's imperative to note that the man comes to Jesus *as a leper.* He doesn't pretend to be anything other than one of the most wounded. He doesn't come to Jesus on his terms, pretending to have control over his life: *"Hey, Jesus. Yeah, I'm good. Family's good, busy at work, you know, the usual. Hey, I wonder if I could bother you about something? I've got things pretty much under control except this one little thing that's making life a bit tough. I could manage on my own, but since you're right here I thought I might as well see if you could do something about it."* Nope. He knows he's a leper and approaches Jesus *as a leper.* His incredible vulnerability leads to honest truth-telling. He makes a plain statement, "Lord, if you are willing, you can make me clean." Amazing truth! But his explicit truth-telling—"You can make me clean"—is made possible by implicit truth-telling—"I am unclean."

The second thing we notice is the trust this man places in Jesus. It's one thing to know you are a leper, to know others know you are a leper, and to live in silence under that truth. It's another thing to stand in front of another human being and say out loud, "I am a leper." What if Jesus wouldn't heal him? What if Jesus did heal him and he couldn't bear feeling his own pain? What if all the pain he had been prevented from feeling all came to him at once? It seems he had an ongoing trust in Jesus. He trusted Jesus with not only his initial healing but also with whatever was to come after.

The last thing we notice is that Jesus gives specific instructions to the healed leper, saying, "'Don't talk about this all over town. Just quietly present your healed body to the priest, along with the appropriate expressions of thanks to God. Your cleansed and grateful life, not your words, will bear witness to what I have done'" (Matt 8:4, MSG). Obeying Jesus' command requires incredible ongoing vulnerability. If the man talks about what Jesus did, he can talk about it in abstract and distant terms. He can get past his past and carry on on his own terms. But a "cleansed and grateful life" ties his story to his acknowledgement of leprosy and his healing from leprosy. We don't know if this healed leper resisted at all, but as emotional lepers, we do. We resist this ongoing act of healing in our lives because with it our lives become about Jesus healing us and not about us controlling or managing our way through life. If there's one thing we like, it's the illusion of being in control. Sometimes we'd rather die of leprosy than give it up.

So what does this story mean for us emotional lepers? We can say without question that we find immense importance in sharing our burdens aloud and having others carry those burdens. Brueggemann says, "the pastoral work has to do with entitling and empowering people to make a case in the presence of God for the legitimacy of their own life." In light of this statement, we remember we are "a royal priesthood" of believers (1 Peter 2:9). We are to carry out this pastoral work for each other, to be the healing hands and feet of Jesus to each other.

Deep friendship centered around a mutual Jesus-like servant heart creates the possibility for trusting vulnerability. As we are the hands and feet of Jesus to each other, we give each other the opportunity to take the first step of dealing with our pain, to kneel in acknowledgment of our emotional leprosy, to utter the truth about our inability to feel our pain. Within that trust we are vulnerably known as ones who has been healed by Jesus. We can lay down all of the identities foisted upon us—president, teacher, drifter, loner, loser, breadwinner, parasite, beauty queen, freak. We can lay down our unrelenting drive to manage our way through life, to live under any labels except "vulnerable." Within that trust we can break the silence, uttering, "heal me, let me feel my pain," knowing those we trust will continue to be there to help us through our pain.

DISCUSSION QUESTIONS

1 As emotional lepers, how have we been taught to mask pain? How do we avoid real solutions by controlling and managing our way through life?

2 Have you ever gone though an experience you felt like you didn't have words to describe? Didn't have people to support you? Do you think our culture makes having genuine relationships difficult?

3 What would it look like to truly share our pain in deep friendship? Is it possible to have true vulnerability among believers? What gets in the way of allowing this vulnerability to take place?

Read Psalm 74 aloud as a public expression.

Psalm 74

Why have you rejected us forever, O God?
Why does your anger smolder against the sheep
of your pasture?
Remember the people you purchased of old,
the tribe of your inheritance,
whom you redeemed—
Mount Zion, where you dwelt.
Turn your steps toward these everlasting ruins,
all this destruction the enemy has brought
on the sanctuary.
Your foes roared in the place where you met with us;
they set up their standards as signs.
They behaved like men wielding axes
to cut through a thicket of trees.
They smashed all the carved paneling

with their axes and hatchets.
They burned your sanctuary to the ground;
they defiled the dwelling place of your Name.
They said in their hearts, "We will crush
them completely!"
They burned every place where God was worshiped
in the land.
We are given no miraculous signs;
no prophets are left,
and none of us knows how long this will be.
How long will the enemy mock you, O God?
Will the foe revile your name forever?
Why do you hold back your hand, your right hand?
Take it from the folds of your garment and
destroy them!
But you, O God, are my king from of old;
you bring salvation upon the earth.
It was you who split open the sea by your power;
you broke the heads of the monster in the waters.
It was you who crushed the heads of Leviathan

and gave him as food to the creatures of the desert.
It was you who opened up springs and streams;
you dried up the ever flowing rivers.
The day is yours, and yours also the night;
you established the sun and moon.
It was you who set all the boundaries of the earth;
you made both summer and winter.
Remember how the enemy has mocked you,
O LORD,
how foolish people have reviled your name.
Do not hand over the life of your dove to wild beasts;
do not forget the lives of your afflicted
people forever.
Have regard for your covenant,
because haunts of violence fill the dark
places of the land.
Do not let the oppressed retreat in disgrace;
may the poor and needy praise your name.
Rise up, O God, and defend your cause;

remember how fools mock you all day long.
Do not ignore the clamor of your adversaries,
the uproar of your enemies, which
rises continually.

Remind each other of God's presence among you, that God can and is willing to heal our emotional leprosy. As a group, try to allow the Spirit to speak, to break the silence, to acknowledge truth.

LEADING INTO LAMENT

If you find yourself a poet, and you wanted to do something like subvert, and bring people to that crisis point of acknowledging their pain, bringing people into pain, how do you do that and still have a job next week?

I think it's not easy, and one has to be wise and not confrontive, but I'm inclined to think that I would let the Bible do some of the work and help people see that biblical texts are so often very elusive, which is evidenced by the fact that we get all kinds of different meanings out of those texts. They don't have one meaning, and I suspect you could almost test this in any local congregation, even if the congregation is very homogenous. People hear it differently, and I'm inclined to think that the hearing it differently is often that we are led by the Spirit to hear it differently.

And I think that what we have to do in most local congregations, I think we have to enlarge the repertoire of Scripture that is available. Most churches I know except the high liturgical churches, people only know about six of the psalms. And those we've learned to read in the flattest, most reassuring kind of way. So I think without pressing it in harsh or abrupt ways, what one can do with the psalms, without taking up the most offensive of them…if you can read a few verses of a psalm and those are verses you couldn't imagine anyone in this congregation ever saying— they wouldn't do that—just ask the interpretive question, who would you imagine could talk like that? Do you know anybody who would talk like that, or have you seen anybody in the news lately that you could imagine talking like that? If you take an angry psalm or something like that, you can imagine that it's a Palestinian mother who is picking up the pieces of her exploded son, or something like that, and has to talk like that.

Latin—it means "in grave or extreme circumstances or at the point of death"

So you begin to open up the sense that because we are human, we all know or can imagine being in extremis. And when we are *in extremis* what we know almost immediately is that our safe, conventional language doesn't quite work. So I think to entertain the thought that in this literature there are voices other than our own that the traditioning process thought were authoritative. And there are people who speak faith in ways other than the way we speak faith, it seems to me, is an important piece of strategy for that.

DISCUSSION QUESTIONS

1 Think about this statement from Brueggemann: "People hear it [Scripture] differently, and I'm inclined to think that the hearing it differently is often that we are led by the Spirit to hear it differently." Do you agree that we hear verses and passages in the Bible differently because we're led by the Spirit to hear them differently? If yes, how can we be sure we're constantly connected to one another so we can learn what the Spirit has to say to us in different ways?

2

Just as John 3:16 seems to have become the tagline of evangelical Christianity, the Psalms seem to be the book we turn to for praise. Why do you think as Christians we know only "about six of the psalms?"

3

Why do you think we avoid psalms of lament? Is it because we can't imagine anyone *really* meaning those words? Because we've never been in extremis? Because we think if we allow ourselves to go there we'll never arrive at praise?

COMMENTARY

The term *in extremis* is a Latin phrase which means "in grave or extreme circumstances or at the point of death." Brueggemann says, "Because we are human, we can all know or imagine being in extremis. When we are in extremis what we know almost immediately is that our safe conventional language doesn't quite work." We've all seen interviews on the evening news with dazed families huddled in front of the smoldering ruins of their home. What do these people say almost every time? "Our house might be gone, but thank God everyone is okay. That's the important thing."

It's always amazing to watch because right there on TV—the same TV that was just trying to convince me the key to my life happiness is yet another advancement in diaper technology—clear, redemptive truth has been spoken. "Thank God everyone is okay. That's the important thing." What amazing truth on the evening news. We know it to be true, which is what makes this scenario cliché: we know that everyone being okay is the most important thing. But it's unfortunate that it takes a crisis for us to act as though it were true.

When I hear these stories, I often imagine the family as they may have been earlier in the day. The father to whoever is nearby, "Who moved my golf clubs? You know I don't like them this close to the freezer." The mother to her daughter, "I've asked you a million times, put the orange juice back in the fridge when you're done." The daughter to her brother, "Stop tapping your foot, I'm trying to study!" In the day-to-day these things do matter; it isn't evil for the father to not want his golf clubs moved too close to the freezer, and really, he's not that annoyed. But these little annoyances have a way of accumulating, of pushing themselves to the front of our minds. They can start to dominate how we see the world around us, to dictate the way we interact with those closest to us. Now, huddled in front of the TV camera, all of those trivialities are, literally, burned away. Things that don't matter usually can't survive when we find ourselves in extremis.

What is true of homes is true of churches. We talk of loving each other, and I believe we mean it. But an accumulation of slights, injustices and annoyances start to dominate how we assume the world works. Our dusty catalog of petty grievances starts to weigh on our interactions with those we call brothers or sisters. Our feelings get hurt when a friend chooses another small group over our own—but we act as if nothing is wrong. We skip Sundays when the associate pastor preaches because his voice is just so grating. And his sermons are too long. And his theology is just a bit flimsy.

I used to work on a dairy farm that also kept a few hens for laying eggs. The hens lived their lives in a wire cage, several hens to each small section. One summer I noticed many of the hens had only a few feathers left—they were bald chickens. I asked my farmer friend if the hens were sick. "Nope," he replied, "they're bored, so they pluck each other's feathers off."

Now, I don't know if my farmer friend was the chicken whisperer and actually knew what those hens were thinking, but that image has stuck with me. Even back then, as a teenager, I remember thinking "That sometimes seems like the church." Jammed together week after week with no real mission or purpose other than to lay the occasional worship egg, we lose sight of "out there," becoming more and more focused on "in here." The more we focus on "in here," the more cramped it starts to feel, and the more listless we become. Pretty soon we're plucking each other's feathers off out of sheer boredom. Until there's a crisis.

Miraculously, when—whether personally or corporately, directly or indirectly—these same bored church goers experience being in extremis, they stop plucking each other's feathers. They respond; they wake up. Ordinary humble people become the very hands and feet of Jesus. Everything that doesn't matter is burned away and the important thing is, is everyone okay? However, in churches as in homes, we are left with the rather pedestrian fact that most of life is not spent huddled in front of one's smoldering home. Most of life is not crisis and drama, and probably a good thing that it isn't.

How, though, do we manage to hold on to what really matters when most of our day-to-day lives are spent dealing with trivial minutiae? This is what Brueggemann is saying; we may not be in extremis, but there are plenty of people who are. We can be reminded of what really matters by being mindful of others, particularly others who are in extremis when we are not. We can be reminded of what really matters by empathetically engaging with others on the basis of our common humanity.

After all, in some ways we are all in extremis. As cliché as it sounds, the mortality rate for humankind is 100% and we are all, in varying ways and to varying degrees, dealing with our own mortality. This is why it's so imperative to be in community with one another. To journey together, listening not only to each other's stories but also to how we view and apply God's story to our own.

Brueggemann suspects we hear the text differently at the leading of the Spirit. While we may not have dire stories, our stories are important because we are all part of humankind. Each story, and each different hearing of Scripture connects us to another facet of being human. Each different hearing is another thread in the rich tapestry of God's story among his people. Each thread which adds to the tapestry of God's story adds to our understanding of God, not as a set of ideas, but as a person revealed in Jesus who moves toward us in love. When we allow it to happen, sharing our stories with one another becomes a theological act.

What if, as Brueggemann suggests, we were to seek out "voices that are other than our own, people who speak faith in ways other than we speak faith" as a strategy for acknowledging pain? For instance, I sometimes wonder how the evening news would be different if it were presented as poetry. Maybe if we engaged poetry rather than "facts," we'd be more prone to enlist our God-given ability to empathize. Maybe if we empathized more often we'd act compassionately more often. Maybe if we acted compassionately more often we'd start to believe we too could receive compassion. Maybe if we started to believe we too could receive compassion, then maybe, just maybe, we might find the courage to acknowledge our pain.

DISCUSSION QUESTIONS

1

Being a part of Western culture, it may be difficult for many of us to believe we have any reason to lament. But we can find ourselves in extremis for many reasons; as stated in the commentary, we're all "dealing with our own mortality." How can being reminded of the temporary nature of life lead us to lament, journey, and *live* with others?

2

Do you agree that hearing Scripture differently from others and sharing our differences "connects us to another facet of being human?" How might allowing other Christians to share their view of Scripture enlarge and benefit our understanding of who God is? How can we create an environment that allows this vulnerable sharing to take place?

3

How is sharing stories a theological act? Can you think of a time when sharing burdens seemed to greater connect you to the story of God?

Read Psalm 137 as a public expression.

Psalm 137

By the rivers of Babylon we sat and wept
when we remembered Zion.
There on the poplars
we hung our harps,
for there our captors asked us for songs,
our tormentors demanded songs of joy;
they said, "Sing us one of the songs of Zion!"
How can we sing the songs of the LORD
while in a foreign land?
If I forget you, O Jerusalem,
may my right hand forget its skill.
May my tongue cling to the roof of my mouth
if I do not remember you,
if I do not consider Jerusalem

my highest joy.
Remember, O LORD, what the Edomites did
on the day Jerusalem fell.
"Tear it down," they cried,
"tear it down to its foundations!"
O Daughter of Babylon, doomed to destruction,
happy is he who repays you
for what you have done to us—
he who seizes your infants
and dashes them against the rocks.

Can you imagine anyone in your neighborhood or city talking like this?

Take another look at verse one: "By the rivers of Babylon we sat and wept when we remembered Zion." Do you know anyone who has especially painful memories?

Read verse four again: "How can we sing the songs of the LORD while in a foreign land?" Who would feel most like an alien and an exile? Is there anyone anywhere in the world you can imagine talking like this?

Read the last verse again (which isn't a metaphor but a description of an actual event): "He who seizes your infants and dashes them against the rocks." Who in the world is most likely to have lost a child to violence?

What might it mean that Psalm 137 ends the way it does?

THE JUICE OF EMANCIPATION

I have just discovered two verses in the book of Exodus in chapter 10 where God says, "I have done all these plagues in order that you may tell your grandchildren about them." So I've been working those two verses… that the whole drama of the Exodus was enacted in order that the grandparents could have something to say to their grandchildren. So, what I wanna say to grandparents like me is your vocation in life is to talk about the juice of emancipation that's been in the world since the Exodus event. And the juice of emancipation is a summons to move out from whoever is the pharaoh of your life. And I think you can work that personally or you can work it systemically about pharaoh. That pharaoh is always the agent of certitude and absolutism and all that, and the news is that we don't owe pharaoh anything.

DISCUSSION QUESTIONS

1

Have you ever stopped to consider
Exodus 10:1-2? How does it make
you feel to think about God taking us
through long, painful journeys so we
can better tell, and hopefully teach,
those who come after us? Does
thinking about this change your opin-
ion of God at all, whether positively
or negatively? How does it affect the
way you think about your responsibil-
ity to those who follow you?

2

How can we begin to determine who, or what, is the pharaoh of our lives? Our society? How can we encourage one another so we can walk through this journey together?

COMMENTARY

This series has moved us on a journey of honestly engaging our pain. In this final video session, Brueggemann acknowledges that our pain is temporary. Through death comes life, through tears come joy. But Brueggemann isn't describing happy optimism that insists everything will turn out rosy. Instead, we can live hopefully, knowing our stories are embedded within God's grand narrative. In God's all-encompassing narrative, which began in Genesis, culminated in Jesus's life and death, and will end upon Christ's return, God is moving to heal his creation. Our individual stories may not have happy endings, but the broader narrative of God's story does. In the end, love wins.

The Jewish notion of *shalom* embraces this idea of hope beyond immediate circumstances. Shalom is often translated as "peace," which we might think of as the absence of personal strife. But shalom is much more than simply a personal state of calm. Shalom is intimate and interior and at the same time broad and encompassing, stretching to include all of creation. It is simple and concise, yet subtle and multifaceted. In an attempt to capture the fullness of the notion of shalom, we could say it is a harmonious completeness. Shalom expands beyond the immediate, to an acknowledgement of God's vast and mysterious plans. It abides in that mystery while trusting in God's goodness. Shalom then rushes inward to our hearts. The mystery of a good and loving God, the mystery of love winning enfolds us and penetrates us to the deepest interior of our being. Thus, we can exist in a sense of harmonious completeness.

Though shalom comes out of the whole story rather than just one chapter, it is as present in the one chapter as it is in the whole story. But we don't have to pretend our sad chapters don't exist or that they're less painful than they are. As a matter of fact, if we live in happy optimism, ignoring the realities of our sad chapters, we miss the chance for hope. Genuine hope comes only amidst hopelessness. If there is "a way out" obtainable through our own power, we don't need hope. Hopelessness has *no choice* but to abide within shalom. Hopelessness must abide within a sense of well-being that comes from the vast mystery of God's story. From within shalom there is hope, not despite our sad chapters but because of them.

Emancipation Juicer

How do we grasp a sense of God's larger story? How can we be reminded of the goodness of God's story despite the sadness of our current chapter? First, we tell specific, contextual, and ongoing stories that reflect and embody God's story—stories of oppression, liberation and redemption.

Stories that reflect and embody the good news: creation was out of right relationship (oppression); God moved to restore creation in the person of Jesus who lived, died, and defeated death (liberation); God's creation is being restored to right relationship, and we are invited into the work of making all things new (redemption). They are stories whose *here and now* is rooted not in circumstances but in relationship, specifically the relationship with creator God, which animates and catalyses all relationships with self, other, and creation. They are stories in which everything about *here and now* is rooted in divine relational reality. They are stories in which everything about *here and now* is rooted in shalom.

By telling stories that reflect and embody God's story, our lens for seeing here and now changes and we see into a God-view of here and now. Once we see into a God-view of here and now, we can live within God's view of here and now. We can live within shalom. When we live within shalom we have experienced the juice of emancipation. Something has come out of our telling of, seeing into, and then living within God's story.

The juice of emancipation will be made up of here and now stories that can then be retold into new stories. It's cyclical but never stagnant because the whole cycle moves within the broader narrative arc of God's story. It returns, but it returns to a new here and now—a new generation, a new people, a new country, a new neighborhood, a new family, a new self.

Brueggemann's closing words are a beautiful way to end this series. They are a benediction rooted in shalom: "The news is we don't owe pharaoh anything." When Brueggemann says we are summoned to move out from "whoever is the pharaoh" of our life, he is referring to the pharaoh of the Exodus story. By "absolutism" and "certitude" he means that literal and, by extension, metaphoric pharaohs operate with a non-God-view of here and now. They see only circumstances and therefore seek to control and manage circumstances. Because chaotic, unpredictable circumstances rarely bend to our control, pharaohs are rarely actually in control. But because they offer a vision of the world in which they are in control, they must speak as though they actually are in control. This leads to absolute and certain talk—there can be no mention of mystery or acknowledgement of pain, only the absolute and certain control and management of immediate and visible circumstances.

In the Exodus story pharaoh speaks in terms that venerate his military power, his wealth and his cleverness. His absolute and certain way of speaking offers a lens through which to see here and now. It is a lens that narrows down and limits future possibility. In pharaoh's vision of here and now, Israel has no power, no wealth, and no cleverness (or technologies, like say, chariots). Through pharaoh's non-God-view of here and now, Israel has zero options, no future hope, no future possibility except in and through pharaoh, who is the sole sustainer and author of future possibilities and thus, future hope.

But the news is there is another lens through which to see here and now. It is God's relational lens of his moving to restore his creation. Through this lens circumstances don't hold sway, relationship does. Specifically, relationship with God. Creator God is the sustainer and author of future possibilities and therefore holds Israel's future hope. Through this God-view of here and now, Israel is loved and treasured and is invited into a shalom view of here and now. Because of God's shalom view the future opens to, literally, infinite possibility.

DISCUSSION QUESTIONS

1 Once the Israelites were free of their pharaoh, they disobeyed God and were made to wander in the desert for 40 years. Do you think we remain under the control of the pharaohs of our lives because we're afraid of what might come next? Afraid to lose the illusion of control? What might it look like to "move out from whoever is the pharaoh of your life?"

2 Brueggemann ends the video with a simple, powerful phrase, "And the truth is, we don't owe pharaoh anything." If we are held captive by a pharaoh in our life, how can we begin to live into the mentality that we indeed don't owe pharaoh anything?

After this five-week study, what are you going to do to embody God's story in your life? To live in shalom?

Read Psalm 126 aloud, as a public expression—
as Israel would have done.

Psalm 126

When the LORD brought back the captives to Zion,
we were like men who dreamed.
Our mouths were filled with laughter,
our tongues with songs of joy.
Then it was said among the nations,
"The LORD has done great things for them."
The LORD has done great things for us,
and we are filled with joy.
Restore our fortunes, O LORD,
like streams in the Negev.
Those who sow in tears
will reap with songs of joy.
He who goes out weeping,
carrying seed to sow,
will return with songs of joy,
carrying sheaves with him.

I remember visiting a family in Cambodia who had received a freshwater well one year before. The well had brought life transforming change to this family. The mother didn't have to spend hours walking to fetch dirty water that would make her children sick. Because the mother could be home and because the children weren't sick, they could go to school. The family was able to irrigate a small garden and grow fresh vegetables. As a result the whole family was stronger and healthier, and by selling some of their surplus, they even earned a bit of money. They were no longer barely surviving; they were flourishing.

Through a beaming smile the mother told us she dreamed of planting flowers next year—simply to enjoy their beauty. Since that day whenever I hear the word "flourish," I think of that family. They still live in a wood and mud hut, they still have virtually no earthly possessions, they are still among the poorest people in the world, but they are flourishing. They have an abiding sense of well-being and, surprisingly, daringly, beautifully, they are dreaming dreams. Simple humble dreams, but they dream dreams.

As you read through Psalm 126, jot down some simple, humble dreams you have. On the other side of the same piece of paper, write down the pharaohs in your life, whether people or attitudes, possessions or ideals that keep you from those dreams. Don't write your list in a self-help, positive thinking kind of way. Be as honest and forthright with yourself as you dare to be. List the pharaohs that insist things will never change, their power cannot be challenged, their rule is everlasting. The pharaohs who won't allow for mystery or pain, who insist on anesthetized control. The pharaohs who must speak in absolute terms and always with certainty lest they lose the illusion of control.

Then, in the middle of paper, between the two lists, write the word "shalom."

Read Luke 7:36-50, preferably aloud and as a group. In the NIV the final word of verse 50 is translated "peace." In Greek the word is *eirene*, which is the New Testament corollary to the Old Testament Hebrew word shalom. Reading the words "go in peace" our Western minds tend to hear, "Go in a state of personal serenity which you manufacture within yourself." We take Jesus's invitation to peace and turn it into an anxious exercise, worrying whether we can attain sufficient levels of peacefulness.

How about this instead?

Go…in peace.
Go…inside of shalom.
Go…knowing you are enfolded within shalom.

As you all leave the safety of your group and step into your, day-to-day here and now, say this blessing together:

You don't owe Pharaoh anything.
Go, knowing you are enfolded within shalom.

NOTES

JOURNEY THROUGH ECONOMY OF LOVE WITH YOUR COMMUNITY:

ECONOMY OF LOVE: SMALL GROUP EDITION
Creating a Community of Enough

A Resource of Relational Tithe

Includes 5 Video Sessions with Shane Claiborne

To order go to thehousestudio.com or economyoflove.org

OTHER RESOURCES FROM THE HOUSE STUDIO:

The Experiment Series unpacks the Sermon
on the Mount, Old Testament practices, and the Ten
Commandments, challenging communities to explore
how life becomes **intentional living** when spiritual
truths and culture collide.

The Kingdom Experiment
*A Community Practice on
Intentional Living*

The Mosaic Experiment
*Bringing Old Testament
Practices Out of Retirement*

WE PUBLISH.
Not because this world needs more books.
Not because the Church needs more resources.
WE PUBLISH BECAUSE GOD IS STILL TELLING STORIES.

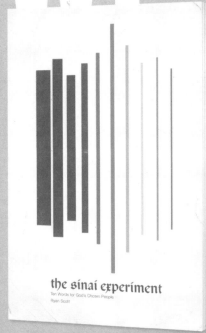

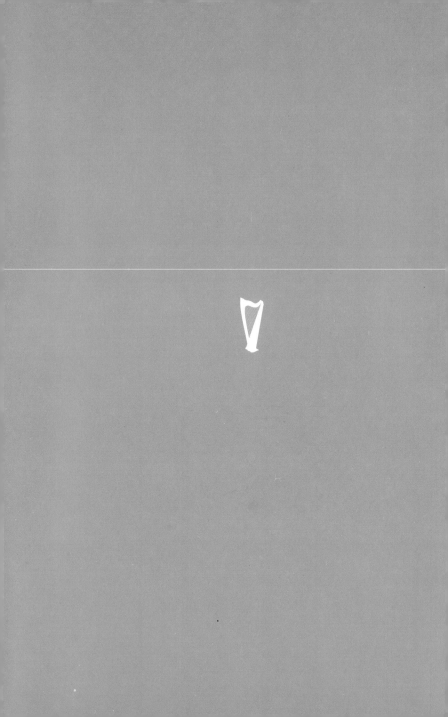